# Sticky Notes
## Harmonizing Affirmations

# Sticky Notes
## Harmonizing Affirmations

### KIM BURRELL

*Noahs Ark Publishing Service*
*Beverly Hills, California*

*Sticky Notes: Harmonizing Affirmations*

ISBN 979-8-9920102-6-8

**Copyright © 2025 by Kim Burrell**

Published by:

Noahs Ark Publishing Service
8549 Wilshire Blvd., Suite 1442
Beverly Hills, CA 90211
www.noahsarkpublishing.com

Creative Concept & Development: Laval W. Belle
Contributing Writer: Sharon D. Hogg
Graphic Design: Christopher C. White

Printed in the United States of America © 2025 All rights reserved. No part of this book may be reproduced or copied in any form without written permission from the author and/or publisher.

*To my mother, Helen Graham Spears,
Thank you for being my encouraging reason to live my best life,
one truth at a time.*

*To Kevin Bernard Jordan,
Thank you for being my first musician, bodyguard and greatest supporter.
I'll forever love and miss you, big brother.*
❤

# FOREWORD

There are moments in life when the noise gets loud—loud with fear, doubt, loss, and unanswered questions. In those moments, what we say to ourselves matters more than we often realize. Words have a way of either weighing us down or lifting us up, either draining our strength or restoring our song.

As a pastor and musician, I've learned that harmony is not just something you hear—it's something you live. Harmony is created when different notes come together with purpose. The same is true with affirmations. When truth, faith, and hope are spoken in unison, they create a sound that steadies the soul. That is what this book, Harmonizing Affirmations, offers: words that don't just speak to your ears, but sing to your spirit.

These affirmations were not written from a distance, but from real life—moments of waiting, wrestling, believing, and pressing forward when quitting felt easier. They are designed to remind you that even when life feels out of tune, God is still composing something beautiful. Every declaration is an invitation to align your heart with hope, your mind with possibility, and your spirit with resilience.

I believe this book written by one of The greatest gospel singers and preachers in America will help you find your rhythm again. Read these affirmations slowly. Speak them aloud. Let them settle into your daily routine like a familiar melody. And when your strength feels low, let these words carry you—reminding you that you are not finished, you are not forgotten, and your best days are still unfolding.

Keep going. Your story is not over yet.

**Dr Mark A Ellis**
Pastor Founder United Christian Faith Ministries Inc

# INTRODUCTION

Music has always been my first language. Long before words formed fully, melodies carried the truths my heart already knew.

Through every season of life—joy, loss, triumph, and transformation—I've learned that harmony isn't found only in music, but in the words we choose to believe and speak. Sticky Notes: Harmonizing Affirmations was born from that truth. Just as a song can shift an atmosphere, a single word spoken in faith can change the rhythm of a day.

These affirmations are "sticky notes" for the soul—simple yet powerful reminders meant to encourage, realign, and bring peace amid life's noise. Rooted in faith and shaped by a lifetime of sound, they are designed to help align what you feel with what you're believing for.

Speak them aloud. Place them where you'll see them. Let them echo until they become movement, faith, and peace.

May these words help you harmonize your voice with your purpose—and sing life into your spirit.

"You're a standing ovation waiting to happen"

"It only takes one moment to have a vacation. It just depends on who you're with."

"Build a life that builds you back"

"I can't pay attention to the past because my present is setting up my future"

"Brilliant minds are not easy to live with... You must qualify."

"Heal fast so you can live again... fast!"

# The heart..
# Grand mama's
# love seat.. ♥

# Don't bore God... Go for it!

Get rid of the you that keeps you from the real YOU...

May Your Well stay Well...

# Free Your Freedom!

# Keep your mind in mind...

# Make peace with peace

Let your body
be a safe place
to live...

Quiet the noise and live out loud!

Your next needs you now...

It's a privilege to be misunderstood when you realize that you were born to be.

All is not lost, hit the reset button...go!

Stay full. What's in the cup is yours. What's in the saucer is theirs...

# I consider you... ♥

I prefer you...

Change your mind and love instead.

# You first...

"Don't allow other people's mindset to define you"

"A blank canvas deserves your dreams painted on it."

Don't lose yourself being the version of you that others created.

# "Be Encouraged... right away."

Be Necessary.

If you're able to notice the wrong... please fix it with what's right.

# Get the Good Out.

"I wish you all of the best"

Save yourself for the moments that need a you...

Moving in silence requires quiet time... you'll be amazed at what you hear.

What comes from the heart reaches everything...

Starve your past... feed the hunger of your future.

# Make your second chance count!...

# Start NOW!... go!

Exercise daily: stretch your imagination... bend your rationale... and build your character... muscle up.

# Winning is losing... but, losing is winning.

Moving in silence should start with what you DON'T say...

Let's check our senses:
Let's See beauty..
Hear hearts...
and Touch lives.

Who knew?
God did.
Now Shine!

Reminder to self... Be alright.

Reminder to self... let it go.

Reminder to self... I'm just fine.

Reminder to self... trust again.

Reminder to self..
LET'S GO!!!

I forgive EVERYBODY.

Believe me...
you MUST
believe in
you ♥

I don't just exist...
I'm necessary.

For Speaking Engagements, Book Signings, Appearances, and Interviews,

Contact:

Michelle Marsden

Phone:

(832) 229-1744

Email:

michelle@iamkimburrell.com

kbcrewbusiness@gmail.com

Website:

www.iamkimburrell.com

Social Media

Facebook: @kimburrelllove

Instagram: @kimburrelllove

Made in the USA
Monee, IL
30 January 2026